# SPARKLING LOVE

## SHREEMATHI

Made with ❤ on the Notion Press Platform
www.notionpress.com

*EMPATH PUBLICATION*

**Sparkling Love**

**-Shreemathi. K. N**

# Contents

# Foreword

*<u>Theme of the story</u>*

*<u>Meeting someone in life is not a coincidence, I think it is destined.</u>*

# Preface

*Falling in love is easy but staying in love is as difficult as holding a hot iron bar with a smile. Here we have Vijay and Janaki falling for each other parting their ways for better reasons yet unable to stay apart as they are not bond by love rather by soul.*

*If love isn't about sacrificing then what else can love truly be. If love isn't about accepting your soulmate with shortcomings then it isn't what you call love.*

# Prologue

*"True love is pure*

*It can make you cure*

*True love arises from heart*

*It won't make you hurt*

*True love is infinite*

*You can't define it*

*True love is in giving*

*Not in demanding"*

*"True love happens at anytime with anyone."*


*He and she:*


*"You can find someone better than me"*


*"No, I can't"*


*"Why?"*


*"Because you are my best"*

# PROLOGUE

# Chapter1

## *SPARKILNG LOVE*

### *1*

*It was a chill morning. The sun was arising from the clouds and the birds were chirping and enjoying the light cool breeze. The dew drops were falling from the leaves of the plants.*

*"Wow!, What a beautiful Sunday morning it is", I looked out through the window and I exclaimed with delight. Taking sketches, pencils, watercolours, papers and stand, I informed my mother and rode to the park at 9:00AM. It was a Sunday routine to paint my heart out. But that Sunday morning I was searching to draw something new. Few minutes later, my eyes captured a scene in the ground and my hands started painting. After completing that*

*painting ( in two hours ), I brought that and walked towards a person who was sitting on a bench and starring at children's playing on that ground. I stood in front of him and called, "Hello sir, Hello… Excuse me". But he didn't respond my call. "Sirrrr", I shouted. He saw me and I grinned. But he turned his face again towards the children playing. The I showed my painting to him. He exclaimed and opened his cute eyes broadly. The reason why he exclaimed was I painted the image of his appearance. I asked him whether he liked that painting.*

*"It's really stunning", He amazed.*

*"Who are you", he asked.*

*"Adheera, studying 12ᵗʰ", I introduced myself. Then I asked his name.*

*"I am Vijay", he answered.*

*I told him that I didn't like that painting. He smiled and asked the reason. "Because this is the first sad painting that I drew", I answered sadly. He smiled cutely again.*

"Can I ask you something?", I asked.

"Ask dear", he said.

"What", I asked.

"Ask", he repeated.

"Sorry", I asked.

"Proceed", he said.

*I told him, "I hear better through others lips than my ears".*

"I am sorry about that", he said.

"It's ok sir", I smiled. Then he turned his face on facing me and said, "Ok, ask your question".

When I painted his face I saw that he had tears in his eyes, sadness on his face, and looked sad all over as he snatched everything away and I asked the reason for his sadness. He simply smiled again.

"Sir, do you know one thing?, you are wearing a cute smile but your sadness masked it. May I know the reason for your sadness behind your tears", I asked kindly. The reason why I asked him that question and worried about him was when I saw him at first a feeling of intimacy appeared in my heart.

He was silent for few seconds. Taking a deep breathe, "Ok, I'll tell... but what will you do after knowing?", he asked me.

*"I'll let your sadness completely away from your heart", I smiled.*

*It was just a words but he felt light when he heard her words.*

*I was very excited to know about him and his past. He started telling his past as a story.*

# Chapter2

2

*The curtains had been wide open, letting the sharp rays of the sun stream in, through the wide open window, on to the face of a cute charming guy Vijay, who was lying on the bed. He stretched slowly and woke up with a fresh mind and smile. Each and every morning and evening, he phoned his family members to speak with them. He loved his family very much. One day when he was talking to them, his parents Lakshmi and Ramachandhiran persuaded him to get married. When they asked about marriage, his one and only answer was "will see". After talking to his parents, young sister Varshini, grand father Govind, grand mother Lakshmi, uncle Krishnan, aunt Priya and their children Teju (10 years old) and Gowtham (5 years old), he ended the call. Then he went to his office at 9.00AM. He had a PA Balakrishnan. When he was returning to his house by his car, there was a huge traffic jam for an hour. During that time, when he was working on his laptop for his office work, someone knocked at his car's window. Once he opened the window a gorgeous girl with her cute smile was standing in front of his eyes. She told him that she was collecting funds for cancer patients and requested him to help them by giving some funds. But he didn't hear her words and was starring at her beautiful eyes and smile.*

*"Sir, sir", his PA called him.*

*"Sirrrrrr", he called him with his full throat.*

*"Sir, she is asking funds for cancer people", he told him.*

*When he gave funds, she thanked him and moved towards another car that was standing next Vijay's car. When she asked funds, there were five men who were inside the car they misbehaved with her and used unwanted words. On hearing that, Vijay stepped out the car and pulled them outside the car.*

"What?... what did you say?", he slapped them and hit them hard. One of the men who misbehaved with her was pushed over the silencer of a bike by Vijay. He screamed and requested him to leave him.

"Ask sorry to her", Vijay said.

"sorry... sorry... sister", asked apology for their behaviour, they stepped inside the car and left from there. "Get lost!", he shouted at them. Then Vijay noticed that she wore a stethoscope and coat and wondered with a confusion why she was asking funds. Suddenly a group of children arrived there and thanked her for helping them.

"Uncle, actually we went to an ashram day before yesterday and there we saw a lot of children in our age who were affected with cancer and certain other diseases, we want to save them. So we are collecting funds now, and knowing about this she offered to help us", one of the children told him.

*"Though you are children by age, you are matured by heart, May God bless you all", he wished them for their doings and he gave more funds to them. One of the children asked him to bend and kissed on his cheeks for his blessed words and gave them more funds. "Thanks my sweetheart", he hugged her. And they turned towards her and thanked for helping them. "That's ok, but please don't come to traffic or any unknown place without a guard", she taught them kindly. Starring at her, he stepped inside the car. He was wordless for few minutes.*

*"What happened sir?", his PA asked him. He smiled and asked him, "Bala, who is she?".*

*"How do I know sir?", he laughed. "Yes, how do you know", he murmured.*

*"But she looked at me like she knew me." He spoke himself.*

*One day later, when he was working with his laptop at night, thoughts of her arose in his mind like a photograph and he wished to see her. He put his face in his two palms and smiled. He was amazed himself for his newly behaviour and for his new born thoughts.*

*The weekend had come. He went outside with his friend Vasu. When he was driving car, chatting with his friend Vasu. He told everything about incident happened in traffic, that time he happened to see that girl near a gift shop whom he saw on that day in traffic. When she entered the gift shop, he parked his car in the parking area and went fast inside that gift shop. Vasu followed him and he didn't know where he was going. Vijay looked for her everywhere in that shop. As he turned towards his right side, in searching of her she appeared in front of him. Vasu asked him what happened and what he was doing there. Then he noticed that he was sighting a girl. "Heyyyy! Vijay, is this you?", he exclaimed about his staring. "she is that gorgeous girl whom I saw her in that traffic", grinned Vijay.*

*Then that day night when he was talking with his family members, someone ringed the calling bell continuously. He ended the call and he moved to the ground floor. When he opened the door, "Viayyyyy!!!!", his friend Karthik and Arjun cried with happiness and they beat him for not talking with them even on phone. "Sorry, sorry... I was busy with some project work", he laughed and said.*

*"For three months!!!!!!!", Karthik kicked him. "That's ok, who have the address and who told you that I am in Chennai?", he asked them. "Last week we went to your home in Coimbatore, and your mother told me that you are in Chennai and we arrived here with Vasu's help", Karthik told him.*

*One hour later, "I got married, Karthik was engaged and Vasu too will be engaged soon, then, what about you Vijay?", Arjun asked Vijay. That time Vasu told about his sighting. "Wow!, who is she", Arjun asked Vijay. "Don't know", he simply said and when he started to tell about that incident that happened in traffic, Vasu closed his ears with cotton. And told them that it was fourth time that he was hearing that. They laughed. Vijay continued to tell that incident.*

*Doo you love her Vijay?", Karthik asked him.*

*"Nothing like that, but... when I remember her, it leaves a smile on my face..., something doing in me!", he smiled. It was 2:00AM, but the conversation had been going without an end. Then they slept at 4:00AM. Next bright morning Karthik and Arjun were ready to leave. Before leaving Karthik gave his wedding invitation to Vijay.*

*"Hey, why didn't you tell this at first yesterday?, Anyways so happy for you, count me in, I'll be there for sure", Vijay wished him.*

*"Don't tell in words, only two weeks more, so both should come before a week", Karthik ordered them. "And it's a love marriage, we will have some more funs", Arjun said.*

*"Love marriage! to you!, oh my God! I don't know what she had done wrong to get lock with you, I think sister is very innocent and pity", Vasu mocked Karthik and they laughed. Then Vijay went to his office.*

*After a week, Vijay and Vasu were ready to go for his friend's marriage to Coimbatore. They went by car. Nearly five days more for Karthik's marriage so they planned to go out and started enjoying their reunion after a long time.*

*One only day more for marriage. So Varsha the bride and her family and friends had come to Karthik's home before a day. Karthik's family welcomed them in a grand manner. Then Karthik introduced Varsha and Varsha's friends to his* friends. Then they made fun filled conversation for almost an hour. That night, Varsha and her friends seemed to be sad.

"What happened to them?", Vijay asked Karthik.

"One of their friends has not arrived yet and her mobile is not reachable, it seems", Karthik told him. "Who is she?", Vijay asked him.

"Janaki Devi", he told her name. When he heard that name he was frozen and had unexplainable feelings arose in his mind. Then he went to balcony and phoned her mother. Few minutes later, Vasu ran towards Vijay and patted his shoulder.

"What happened Vasu?"

"Come with me Vijay, a shocking surprise waiting for you", Vasu pulled Vijay to garden. When he went there, he was surprised to see her again whom he met in traffic and took her breath away for few *seconds.*

*"Hello... Hello... Vijay", her mother was on call.*

*"Amma, I'll call you later", he ended the call.*

*Janaki came in front of him like an angel and seeing her again was like a fantasy to him. She was talking to Varsha's friends.*

*"Hey Karthik! Who is she?"*

*"She is Janaki, they were waiting for her before."*

*"Vijay... Vijay..., I'll tell this to our friends", Vasu murmured in Vijay's ear.*

*"No, this is not a right situation to have conversation about this, we will speak about this later", he grabbed Vasu's hand.*

*Sitting as a group Karthik and his friends, Varsha and her friends started a conversation about love.*

*Vasu told them, "To marry a girl, boys should respect, honour and love her, then only girls will be impressed. Above all we should wait until she tells her love. To boys, the girls smile is enough, when girls smile at us, our game is over and we will fall in love and really don't know what they add for their smile".*

*"It's a sad universal truth." Karthik and friends started laughing.*

*On hearing that, Vijay seated centre among them.*

*"Enough Vasu, it's not like that", he asked them to stop laughing. "Why?"*

*"Hmm, I'll ask you a question, Do you know why do girls love their fathers to the core?".*

*Everyone started thinking.*

*"Ok, let me tell you, the reason why daughters love their fathers the most is at least one man in the world who will never hurt her and love her take care of her, honour her and give respect to their daughters. They feel safe in their hand. That kind of protection, she can't feel suddenly with any men or if you tell your love to her. If you love a girl, you should have some patience until she feels safe in your hand. It may take also years to feel that protection in you. You know why, only 21 to 24 years she will be with her family, after that, life long, she will be with you. For that there is nothing wrong to wait for her, give some space to them to think".*

*Everyone applauded him to hear his words.*

*"Wow! Vijay, but how do you know this?", Arjun asked.*

*"Hey, I have a young sister like an angel, you know that right?", He asked him.*

*"Yes"*

*"She said this once, there I came to realize".*

*"She is blessed!", Fathima murmured.*

*"Who?", Janaki asked.*

*"His future partner".*

*That time, her smiley face became sad thinking of something and left to room. Vijay noticed her sad face and her leaving to room. Next morning Janaki went to bride's room.*

*"A new life, new responsibilities and a sweet chapter of your life will be begun today in few minutes. May you always stay together in love and understand each other more", she wished her and gave a gift to her.*

*"Thank you Janu", Varsha hugged her.*

*"Hmm, be happy forever!"*

*The marriage happened grandly and happily in temple and they returned home afternoon. Janaki was standing alone in balcony and starred at the sky with tears at night. On seeing her tears, Vijay felt sad. Though he wanted to move towards her to ask, something jammed him. In that moon light, she looked more beautiful to his eyes.*

*"She is such a competitive to the Moon's beauty".*

*Next day morning he met Varsha and asked the reason for Janaki's tears and noticed that Janaki was pretending to be happy and though she spoke to everyone with a smile and love, he felt her smile seemed to be fake. She and her friends Fathima, Jeni didn't know why he was asking about her suddenly. Vasu, Karthik and Arjun were also there.*

*"Karthik, when we went to Vijay's house at Coimbatore, that day he said that he saw a girl in a traffic... gift shop and he was impressed by her... it is none other than your wife Varsha's friend Janaki", Vasu made them remember.*

*"What!! Janaki is that girl.", exclaimed Karthik and Arjun.*

*"Hey!! Vijay, do you love her?", Fathima asked him. "Don't know, but... something is doing in me when I see her!", he smiled.*

• 21 •

*Varsha and her friends started telling about Janaki's past life.*

# Chapter3

**3**

*Janaki, Jeni, Fathima and Varsha were best friends from 9ᵗʰ standard. They had been studying together from 8ᵗʰ standard. Janaki was an intelligent girl and was the topper of the school. She helped her friends to pass the exams in distinctions. After, 10ᵗʰ annual holiday, they stepped into 11ᵗʰ standard in that same school. Few days later, Jananki came school sadly and her friends didn't know why she was sad and Janaki didn't tell anything to them. So Varsha, Jeni and Fathima went to her home. Janaki was sitting in garden area. When they went near, they saw her eyes were red. They were frightened to see her like that. When they asked the reason for her sadness, tears burst out from her eyes. Fathima wiped her tears and hugged her. Then they asked the reason for her sadness. She told them that her father was busy with his business work and came home once in a blue moon and he had been fighting with her mother without any reason and added that her father came two days before with a divorce notice and asked her mother harshly to sign in that paper. But she didn't sign in that paper, so he slapped her and went angrily. Her friends worried to hear that. Janaki's mother Dhakshayini was kind hearted, lovable and sweet woman, but they didn't know why her father Raghavan behaved like that. Janaki too didn't know the actual reason. Next day, Janaki came school normally and concentrated on her studies. On seeing that, her friends felt happy. Janaki secured 1ˢᵗ place in 11ᵗʰ and 12ᵗʰ as usual and also her friends secured topper rank in 12ᵗʰ. She also received award for "The best student of the year" for two times.*

*Janaki loved her mother very much and was everything to her. She always made her mother smile and happy. One day, when Janaki was playing with her mother, Aravind who was elder brother to Janaki, returned home after completing his Master's degree.*

*"Aravind!!", Janaki and Dhakshayini mother exclaimed with joy and hugged him. Tears welled up from his eyes and he was so happy to see them after a long time. His sister was a little princess to*

*him. He congratulated her for her achievements in her studies and awards and gifted her a car. She exclaimed with joy for his gift. When they had their lunch in afternoon, Aravind asked Janaki, Is he still fighting with our mother?"*

*"Who?", she asked.*

*"Who else?", he said.*

*"Our father?", she asked.*

*"Hmm", he said.*

*"No, and... he will come next month.", she lied as mother Dhakshayini asked her to tell Aravind if he asked anything about father. Aravind did not like his father, as he did not show much care on family.*

*One day, in afternoon her mother asked Janaki to come outside with her to eat ice cream as Janaki felt bored. Aravind was busy with his work in laptop so he couldn't go with them. That time, Fathima arrived there. Together, they went out to eat ice cream. Only six days more for Janaki's birthday so her mother wished to gift her something special. She asked them to stay there in that ice cream shop and she would return in few minutes. Her mother saw a gift shop which was opposite to that ice cream shop. She crossed the two roads and entered that shop. Half an hour has gone, but Janaki's mother had not returned yet. So Janaki and Fathima came out from ice cream shop to see where she had gone. When Janaki's mother was trying to cross the second road, a heavy vehicle came fast that time.*

*"Aunty, careful", Fathima shouted. In a fraction of second, that heavy vehicle hit Janaki's mother and threw her in front of Janaki's eyes.*

*"Ammmaaaaaa!!!!", she screamed and rushed out near her.*

*"Oh my God! Aunty"*.

*"Amma, Amma, look at me Amma!"*, she requested her with tears and shock. Her mother floated on blood. When she saw that blood Janaki's heart was beating fast and she was frightened. She held her mother's hands and cried to see her. The suffocation did not stop.

*"Fathima, call Aravind"*, she cried.

*"Aravind... Amma!"*, Janaki's words stammered.

*"J... J... Janaki"*, her mother called her and looked at her with a smile and died in her lap. Her hand fell down from Janaki's hand. She was frozen for a few seconds.

*"A... A... Amma"*, tears came from her eyes like a flood.

*Aravind cried through the call where they were and what happened. He rushed out and searched them everywhere. He saw a crowd on road and went inside with a fear. He was shocked to see her mother like that. He knelt down and held her hands with tears in his eyes, he shouted, "Ammmaaa".*

*Two days later, Aravind asked what really happened between their father and mother and also asked why they could not reach him even by phone call. Janaki told the truth to her brother. On hearing that Aravind got angry over his head on his father. Suddenly Janaki remembered the incident when her mother was crossing the road, Janaki saw that her mother was shocked looking at her phone. She felt something was in phone and immediately opened her mother's phone. His father sent a photo, when Janaki opened that, she was also shocked like her mother. He sent a photo that he had married a rich woman. Then she came to know that why her father asked to sign in divorce paper. When she showed that photo to his brother, he was angered over his head. And they realized that the photo was the reason for her shock and made her cross the road without watching two sides. Aravind decided to take her sister abroad with him. Three days later, it was her birthday. She went near her mother's photo.*

*"Amma, today is my birthday, wish me Amma!", her words stammered with tears. "Amma, I want to hear your voice, please come and talk to me Amma, I can't live without you", she knelt down in front of her mother's photo and cried. On seeing her tears and hearing her words, Aravind couldn't bear and his eyes became watery.*

*Later, she went to her room and saw a cover which was brought by her mother on that day road accident. She opened that cover, she saw a gift box, on that gift box, "Happy birthday my daughter!" was written and when she opened that, she saw a statue of a mother hugging her daughter, she kissed that statue with tears. She saw a "J" lettered silver bracelet and wore it.*

*she smiled with tears.*

*"I love you Amma"*

*The next day, their father came home and went to his room and was searching some documents. On seeing him, Aravind pushed him down and scolded him. There was a jostle between them. His father pushed Aravind on the staircase. He was hit by staircase on the backside of his head and fainted. Taking the documents, he left home. "Anna, Anna, get up!", she sprinkled water on his face with fear. "I'm ok, don't worry", he woke and relaxed her. At night, he went to sleep with an unbearable pain on his back head. Next morning, Janaki went to wake him up.*

*But she couldn't find any movement from him.*

*"Aravind... hey, Aravind", she patted on his cheeks with a shock. His body was so chill, he even did not have breathe. She came to know that he had died. "You too left me Aravind!" Why did you leave me Anna?, you said that you would be with me", she hugged and cried badly. Days went, she couldn't bear Aravind's death and felt alone without her*

*mother and brother. In her cuboard She wanted to move on for her studies and she thought only that could give a relief to her. Packed her things and joined Ramachandhiran college in Coimbatore luckily her friends Varsha, Jeni and Fathima too had a seat in that same college. When she was in second year, Ajay who was studying in same class, always forced and tortured her to accept his proposal, but she did not mind his doings. One day, his torture to the extreme level. "Don't you understand what I am saying, I want to study, Just leave me", she slapped him. Ajay got angry on her and harshly told her that he would never leave her.*

*Years have passed. As they wished, they completed their studies and became doctors. At first, Janaki went to work in Chennai, but she did not feel comfortable and her mother and brother's thought often came in her mind and made her cry. She remembered when she was child, her mother told that her grandparents house was in Coimbatore. She went and stayed there permanently.*

# Chapter4

4

*On hearing her hurtful past, Vijay and his friends were wordless. One day he asked why she was always sad. Knowing her painful past, a Professor named Mr. Krishnan, who was kind hearted helped her and took care of her like a father to complete her studies without any trouble.*

*"He is none other than younger brother of Vijay's father". Karthick said.*

*"What a twist here!", Fathima exclaimed.*

*"Yes, it is his father's college only".*

*They were shocked and excited to hear that.*

"VK Company... Mr. Ramachandhiran...", Varsha was thinking...

"Yes, what you are thinking is right, He is the son of VK company's owner Mr. Ramachandhiran". Karthik said.

They were so happy to meet him.

"But the truth is... She did not like business people, that's only because of his father". Fathima said sadly.

"Don't tell anything about me to her. Let me handle this and take care of her.", He gave trustful words.

Vijay asked them whether her grandparents were there. Fathima told him that she was alone in that house and her grandparents were no more.

*Next day, Vijay returned to his home in Coimbatore. After chatting with his family members and had dinner with them, he went to his room. By remembering her hurtful past, he wished to take care of her more.*

*One evening, when he was returning home from his office by his car, he phoned Karthik to ask Janaki's house address. When phone was ringing, he saw some men was chasing Janaki in the street and she was trying to escape from them. Parking his car in the corner of the road, he ran towards them and fought with them to save her. He hit them and saved her. Then, he asked the reason for their chasing but she refused to answer. "Tell me Janaki", he shouted.*

*One week before she saw her neighbour Megna who was 17 years old, talking with a man at night under the tree which was opposite to her house for two days. She went there and asked who he was and warned them that she would never see him with her again. Once he left that place, Janaki asked Megna about that guy. She told her that he was her friend Srinisha's elder brother Bavan and they loved each other. She got angry to hear that. As she felt something was not good with him, she advised and order her to focus only on her cricket practice and not to talk with him thereafter. Megan told Janaki that he had told her that he would take care of her like a queen and loved her more. "Idiot, don't believe his words", she shouted didn't know how to explain that he was not good.*

*Megna was a good cricket player and her coach told her that if she worked hard daily, in few months she would be selected under 18 to play in state level. Her parents financially poor and she was a single child to them and they were working hard to earn money for her daughter's life and goal. So Janaki requested Megna to remember her parents and concentrate more on playing cricket. She said, "ok Akka".*

*Two days later, Bavan and some men were trying to pull Megna inside the car. When Janaki stepped into that street she saw them. "Megnaaaa!", she was shocked and panicked. When Bavan took an acid bottle to pour on Megna's face, Taking pepper spray from her handbag, she ran towards and sprayed on them. "Megna, don't fear, come with me", they ran and escaped from them. After that incident, Megna didn't continue her practicing and disturbed mentally. Janaki requested her parents not to let their daughter outside for some days. They worried about their daughter's doing. She filed a complaint against Bavan and his friends in police station. That day evening, when she left from hospital, a group chased her and warned her to get back her complaint and they threatened her that if she didn't get back, they would kill her and Megna. To save Megna's future, she got back the complaint but she didn't know even after getting the complaint back why they were chasing her but they were new men then.*

*Hearing her words, "Ok, don't worry... I'll do something to solve this problem", Vijay said. He saw an injury above her eyebrow, when he touched with his fingers, "Ahh!", she felt pain. Vijay took her home safely and first aided her injury.*

*"Thanks", she said*

*"Need not", he replied. He asked whether she didn't fear when she gave complaint.*

*She smiled.*

*"What? tell me", he asked.*

*"Actually no, because I don't have parents or anyone in my life so", she gave a worried smile. Vijay got angry when she told him that she didn't have anyone and deep down he knew that he would always be there for her.*

*"Where do see Bavan often?", he asked her.*

*"He and his friends are mostly in a ground which is in the corner of the street.", She said.*

*One morning, Vijay went to Megna's home. Her parents were sitting in the floor.*

*Who are you?", they stood.*

*"Can I meet Megna?, Vijay asked.*

*"There is no one called Megna here"*

*"I am Janaki's friend"*

*"Get in."*

*Megna was sitting in the corner of that room with tears in her eyes.*

*"Megna!"*

*"Who are you?", she was scared.*

*Vijay flashed a video on Megna's face.*

*"Get up and come with me, if you trust me"*

*They both went to an abandoned old factory. Megna became anxious on seeing the seen in reality than in video. In that factory Bavan and his friends were beaten up nicely and tied with rope.*

*"What do you want to do to them?"*

*"No... No... Nothing".*

*Holding her hands, "If you had had an elder brother, would he have left you to cry like this?", he asked.*

*"Anna... Just, leave them", she said firmly.*

*"What... But why?"*

*"Bavan has a younger sister, and she is my best friend, she loves her brother to the core and if she knows that her brother is not a good human and if something wrong happens to him, she won't be able to bear", she said sobbing. Vijay was amazed at her words and went near to Bavan.*

*"Forgiving you is the biggest punishment that you ever get and this will kill the spirit within you.", Vijay let them go from there. Her forgiveness made them to realize their mistakes and Vijay's words kept hovering in their ears. Bavan moved out without raising his head.*

*"Megna, Shall we move now?", Vijay held her hand. While he was driving the car, Vijay gave a hope to her that they would not disturb her thereafter. Suddenly, tears burst out from her eyes.*

"*Hey, What happened, Are you worrying that you have done mistake?*", *he asked kindly.*

"*Yes anna*", *she cried.*

"*Ok cry, as much as you want. But Megna, you should know one thing that you have not done anything wrong, your one and only mistake was believing that person. In this teenage, whatever you see it attracts, whatever you hear, you trust and whomever you meet you believe them. This teenage makes you think like you know everything. But it is not. This thought made you to suffer as you have suffered now. So don't let your mind to trust anything or anyone when you see newly and everything you see is not real. Only two things are real, one is your parents and other is your goal. These two only come with you lifelong and make you to grow. So just come out from that incident and concentrate on your goal, make your parents proud and happy. Look, a big crowd is waiting in the stadium to see you playing in near future*". *Vijay motivated her as much as he could.*

"Ok anna, surely I'll make my parents proud", she said and wiped her tears. When they reached home, she went inside her home with tears. "Sorry Amma, sorry Appa, forgive me... I'll not do any mistakes hereafter", she cried and hugged them. They were happy to see her like that. They told him that they had one child and she was a good girl. When she was mentally sick after that incident happened, they were scared that they would lose her, but he arrived like a God and saved their child. They thanked him.

Few days later, Janaki had a call from unknown number. "Hello, who's that?", she asked.

"Janaki!!! I am Vijay", Vijay replied.

"Hey, Vii", she paused.

*"Which Vijay, I don't know who you are", she ended the call up.*

*In an hour Vijay went her house and asked why she answered him that she didn't know him.*

*"what!!, Have you called me", she asked.*

*"Yes", he replied.*

*"Ok cool, I just played", she grinned.*

*"What!! Playing!!", suddenly he searched something to beat her. With laugh she ran inside her house and Vijay followed. They started to play like children. He tried to catch but she escaped. Vijay was happy to hear her laughing sound.*

*"Hey wait, how do you know my number?", Janaki asked with a confusion.*

*"If you want to know, come with me", he had a surprise for her.*

*She didn't know where he was bringing her and asked him. She didn't know what the surprise was until she saw Megna in play ground. She was surprised to see her in that ground. Megna and her coach thanked Vijay for bringing back to that ground. Janaki hugged her with happiness and wished her to achieve in her life. "Akka, I thought to meet you in your house before coming to the ground, but suddenly I wished to see you here and told him so he brought you here. And I gave your number to him", she said.*

*"Ok dear, I am so happy to see you here!", Janaki smiled. Megna went near to Vijay.*

*"Thanks Anna", tears filled in her eyes.*

*"It's, ok dear, everything will be alright, look... past never determines your future when you think about*

the past, you can't move and change anything so avoid thinking about the past, focus on present to make your future bright and achieve more!", he wiped her tears and gave strength to her.

"Ok?", he asked

"Ok!!", she said.

"Present is the only key to lock your hurtful past and unlock your bright future", his words gave strength to her and she stepped inside the ground started practicing.

Then they left from there.

"Hey, were you surprised?", Vijay asked while driving the car.

"Really surprised!!!!", she was amazed.

*"But I could never believe that she had come back to play ground!!", she wondered.*

*Vijay smiled and said "You know what, it is not her mistake, it is the age to believe everything she sees, she hears and she is so kind-hearted in nature that's why she believed his words blindly".*

*He said to her, "This age causes over trust, over trust causes over care, over care causes over love, over love causes over thinking and it leaves a person broken at the end".*

*Most of the people have lost their lives in this age by doing*

*these mistakes. If a daughter or a son does anything without telling to their parents in between 17 to 20 ages, it ends in tragedy only... not for everyone, but most of the cases". She was impressed and amazed with his words.*

*"Ok, what is real love?", Janaki asked.*

*"Real love never needs often meetings or attraction between two souls... less communication but deep conversation, less meeting but beautiful memories, this is my thought about love". He smiled at her. She was dumb struck to hear his words and told him with a smile that he really spoke well. Few seconds later, "You are so cute when you smile", he told her. "My mother often told me", she said. "Your mother did not leave you alone, she has been living in your smile, so smile always!", he said. Hearing his words she felt a sparkle in her heart but it was inexpressible and she became silent until they reached her home.*

*Days passed by. One night, it was near 11:00PM, when she stepped outside the hospital, she was frightened to go alone to her home. She felt someone was following her. Suddenly she thought of Vijay, when she took phone to call him, "Hello... Doctor...", Vijay called from her left hand side. "Vijay!!", she was surprised. He had a work in his office and it took more time to complete and when he crossed that hospital,*

*he thought to see her and waited for her. "what are you doing here?", she went near and asked him. "Waiting for someone?", he said. "for whom?", she asked. He went closer to her ears.*

*"I am waiting for a girl who is standing in front of me and asking question!!, he smiled at her. With a hidden love smile he went near his car and stepped inside the car.*

*While Vijay was driving the car suddenly got breakdown. It was one kilometre to reach her home. Then they started walking.*

*"Do you feel ok to walk at this time on this road?"*

*"Yes", she said. "Don't you have fear?", he asked. "Why should I fear when you are next to me?..., I*

*don't have fear", she said and walked forward. He exclaimed to hear her words.*

*Few seconds later, "Who am I to you and what do you think about me?", Vijay asked Janaki. "My friend", she said.*

*"Only friend?" He asked.*

*"Then?", she asked. Suddenly a man with a knife ran towards Vijay and tried to stab him. "Vijay, carefull!!", she panicked and fainted. That time a few men came and surrounded him to kill him. But at last they were hit badly by Vijay and they escaped from him. Vijay took her in his arms and moved to her home. Around 11:00PM, Janaki suddenly came to her conscious and screamed "Vijayyyy".*

*"Hey, I am hear, chill", he relaxed her. Vijay, Vijay are you ok?", she hugged him with a fear. "I am alright", he consoled her and offered her some coffee.*

*"What happened last night?"*

*"They were trying to attack us, but I don't know who they were. Then as you were fainted, I took you in my hands here".*

*Suddenly Janaki saw his back shoulder bleeding.*

*"Vijay! Remover your shirt", She panicked.*

*"What!"*

*"Remove it I said"*

*"Vijay!, Your shoulder is injured", She searched the first aid kit.*

*"Hey! Nothing, it's just a small injury."*

*"Close your mouth first, See What is in my hand",
She said by keeping scissors near his mouth.*

*"Ishhh! It's paining", he screamed.*

*"Small... injury!" she glared.*

*As he felt sleepy, he laid down on her lap and slept
peacefully.*

*She patted his head and bent near his ears and said,
"Thanks for being with me". At once he held her
hands near his chest and slept like a child.*

*Sun has arisen, birds were chirping.*

*"Vijay! Get up, it's 8:00AM".*

*"Five minutes mommy".*

*"Mommy!", she laughed.*

*Slowly he rubbed and opened his eyes and saw Janaki.*

*"Janaki! When did you come to our home?"*

*"Idiot, wake up and look around. Did you lose your memory?", she laughed.*

*Vijay came to his conscious and laughed. Soon after he had breakfast, he moved from her house to office at 9:00AM.*

*At 11:00AM, she texted him, "Can you come and pick me at 9:00PM?"*

*"Sure!" he replied. After seeing his text, with a smile she started doing her work in hospital.*

*Vijay went to the hospital at sharp 11:00PM to picked her up. Once she stepped inside the care, she slept as she was exhausted.*

*He slowly stopped the car once he reached her house. She didn't wake. Slowly he moved his hand towards her face and moved her hairs to her backside of her ear.*

*"No need to thank me, I'll always be with you!", his eyes was full of love.*

*She gradually woke up and saw him.*

*"Where are we?"*

*"Turn and see", he showed her house.*

*She stepped outside the car and when she about to enter the home, she stepped back and turned towards him. She looked and smiled at him.*

*"What?", he looked at her.*

*"Come here", said Janaki'.*

*He went near her and at once she hugged him. He was numb and he could not express his happiness.*

*"Be with me till my last breath, don't go away from me.", She cried.*

*"Stop crying, I won't leave you alone, I am with you only", he wiped her tears and kissed her on her forehead.*

*"Good night, Vijay".*

*"Sweet dreams".*

*As she was in a trouble, when she travelled alone to her home, most of the times he always stood after the two house from Janaki's house. He waited until she came to her house safely. After seeing her only, he moved to his house.*

# Chapter 5

5

*It was one Sunday morning. When he got up from his bed, he decided to confess his love to her. But he was scared whether something would happen wrong, if she came to know the truth about him.*

*That time he heard a loud noise from his father. He came to dinning hall to see him. He was dancing happily.*

*"What happened Appa?"*

*"Third time our company reached the top first place of all".*

*They were so happy to hear that.*

*The following day, there was an award function for his success. Vijay arrived there earlier from his office.*

*"Congrats Appa... Where is Krishnan Uncle?"*

*"He is on the way"*

*While they were conversing happily, Vijay had a phone call from his PA and he moved from that place. When he came towards his place, he saw his uncle had arrived and was talking with his family members, he also noticed that they were talking to a girl, as they were standing in a group he could not see her face clearly except her hands and ears. Her voice only heard to his ears among the big crowd and it was much familiar to him. He was moving near them with heart beats.*

*Suddenly, his uncle turned and called, "Hey Vijay, come here".*

His heart was about to burst and his eyes were frozen, once he saw that girl was none other than Janaki.

"Vijay, come here, Why are you standing there?"

He was shocked to her.

"Vijay, She is Janaki Devi, one of my best students, I met her in a shop in the morning after a long time. And Janaki this is Vijay"

"Hai Vijay!", with a smile she shook his hands.

He thought everything was over and that meeting was the end card to his love for her as she came to know that he was the son of a business man and she would not accept his love if he proposed her.

*He was wordless and he sat on his seat. Vijay's father was requested to come on the stage to receive the award. On that stage, he happily said that the award was dedicated to his son Vijay as he was the major reason for his success. Vijay's eyes turned to see Janaki. She was laughing and applauding happily.*

*The Sun was about to set. Janaki was sitting on a sea shore and starring at the sea and Sun. Vijay arrived there with tension.*

*"Hey Vijay, come sit".*

*"Janaki... I... I am sorry... Sorry for..."bent his head.*

*"I know what you are trying to say now", she smiled.*

*"Did I ever ask who you were?".*

*"No"*

*"I never asked anything about you and so you never told me, let it be that way itself. ". Her words made him think about the past and he realized that she did not ask anything about him.*

*"But, Why?", he was confused.*

*She took a deep breath and smiled. She was quiet for few seconds.*

*"Vijay... Shall I tell you one thing?".*

*"What?"*

*"Vijay... Our marriage was already decided one when I was 17".*

*"Janakiiiii"*

*"Yes Vijay, after completing my schooling. I was on my holidays. One days my mother's friend visited our home after a long time. They both were best friends during school days and they were so happy to get together after so many years. My mother introduced me to him. He talked to me and played with me. Then they were talking about their school days and family nearly two hours. I noticed that he was so happy to meet my mother. My mother also forgot about our family issues, when she talked to him. When he was about to leave, he told her that their beautiful friendship should remain forever. He asked my mother whether I could be his daughter-in-law in future". She smiled and told him, "Sure, if time permits". He blessed me and left.*

*"Janaki! What are you going to say as conclusion?", he was literally confused.*

*"My mother's friend is none other than your father Mr. Ramachandhiran".*

*"What!", he exclaimed.*

*"Yes Vijay!"*

*He was surprised to here that.*

*"Then"*

*"Then... There is one more thing"*

*"What is that Janaki?"*

*She went near his ears and said "I Love You".*

*" Vijay, I never let anything to be more important in my life after my mother and brother were dead. The thing which I considered more important than anything in my life that would not stay with me forever, I am afraid Vijay".*

*Vijay was on cloud nine. Suddenly he turned and knelt in front of her.*

*When he was about to express his feelings, a group of men arrived near them, and hit Vijay with a rod.*

*"Vijayyyyyy", she screamed.*

*"Who are you all? Why are you coming again and again?"*

*That time, a guy who was behind that group came in front of them.*

*"Bavan!!!!!", Janaki' shocked.*

*"Do you remember me Janaki?"*

*"Vijay, I have tried to kidnap her, but you saved each and every time. So I decided to kill you first"*

*"But why"*

*"I have been loving her from college times and I wanted her to be mine, but she ignored me".*

*"Bavan, please... enough... stop torturing me, I beg you... please leave us!", she cried.*

*Bavan moved his foot towards Janaki and tried to pull her inside the car.*

*Vijay got angry over his head and they started fighting. While they were for fighting, his back head was hit and he fell down. He was half fainted. But he never stopped hitting them. All ran away from that place. But Bavan hit him hard and with glass bottles he hit Vijay's face and he got hurt in his eyes. The blood was drooping all over the shore, he fell down and lost his conscious. On seeing him like that, Janaki's heart almost ripped into pieces.*

*When Bavan came closer to her, she took her pepper spray and sprayed in his eyes and hit him and started moving to save Vijay.*

*She took him and drove the car to hospital. She was afraid that he was going to disappear from her life. She never thought that she would see him in that state.*

# Chapter6

*6*

*After a month, Vijay got his consciousness and he opened his eyes slowly. All his family members and friends were there in front of him. But her eyes searched for Janaki.*

*He went to many places and searched her as much as he could. But she was nowhere. He was broken.*

*"Standing in front of the mirror*

*Looking at my face on it with tears*

*Hating myself*

*I can't even accept your leaving!*

*I feel alone, I don't know why!*

*Here I have locked my room, lying on the floor and thinking about you and missing you right now more than anything. I feel this is really the worst and most painful part of our story!*

*Ahhh!"*

*The voice of his longing for her echoed over the world.*

*"Where are you Janaki?*

*Even though I have eyes to see, I became blind without knowing the way to you.*

*Since the day you left me*

*Thinking of the memories you had with me makes my heart happy*

*But the mind is saddened that it has disappeared as mere canal water*

*Happiness and sadness play on me in the same line*

*Why did my voice of sadness go unheard?*

*Even though I was in a peaceful place, I found that my mind had turned me into a warlock*

*Don't let your memories kill me*

*Wandering like a threadless kite*

*When will you hold me with your fingers,*

*Waiting for you*

*But even if the feet of the seeker are worn out, they will not stop looking for you!"*

*He went out and continued searching her.*

# Chapter7

7

*"Three years have gone. But still she is not found. Day after tomorrow is her birthday." Vijay's eyes filled with tears.*

*"What is it like without her?", I asked.*

*"It's... it's aching!"*

*"Her absence... It neither let me live nor let me die."*

*He started crying. On hearing his hurtful past I could not breathe as I felt that pain.*

*It pierced my heart like anything and I cried along with him.*

*"It's okay, I'll be alright Adheera. It's already late. Go home, we will meet another day".*

*"Do you have her photo?"*

*"Yes", he searched his phone in his pocket.*

*"I kept my phone in my room".*

*"See this is my number, you can catch me anytime, if anything is needed."*

*"When are you departing from this town?", asked Adheera.*

*"I'll be here for two days".*

"*Ok*".

"*Bye dear, take care*".

*I returned home with heart full of sadness and pain. I didn't even talk to my mother.*

*Next day morning, after having my morning breakfast I talked with my mother.*

"*Adheera, yesterday Janani came and asked me why you did not come to her home*".

*Janani Akka was my neighbour and she had been staying there for two years. She only taught me sign language, lip reading and she was helping me with my studies also.*

"*Yeah I forgot Amma, I'll go this evening*".

In the evening I went to her home. She was making sweets to sell. As she was visually challenged I often went to help her.

"Akka!", I hugged her.

"Don't talk to me".

"Sorry Akka, I was busy in drawing pictures".

"Ok"

"Could you bring the scissors? I kept upstairs".

"Sure"

I went upstairs and searched for scissors. That time I saw box under the bed. When I pulled out and opened that box, I saw a statue of a mother kissing *her daughter and a key chain. I remembered mother Dhakshayini's present to Janaki which was said by Vijay. Then I turned back and I saw the wardrobe was unlocked which was usually locked. I saw some files were there. When I opened that file I read the name "Janaki Devi". Her school and degree certificates were there. When I related this to that story, I realized that Janani was Janaki Devi. I was shocked and wordless.*

*I went down and stood at her back and asked,*

*"Is Janani your real name?"*

*I saw her hands froze and she stood as a statue when I asked that question.*

*"Akka"*

*She turned and said "What doubt in that?, Why are you asking suddenly?"*

"When did you lose your eyes?"

"I already told you that I lost my eyes in an accident."

Akka... But...

"Stop asking these many questions, tomorrow is my birthday you know that, I am going to serve sweets to children in Church like I did it in last two years."

"Yeah!"

I confirmed that she was Janaki.

I rushed out to my room. I was messaging continuously, and made calls, he did not come to line. I was scared whether he was leaving the town.

*At 11:00PM I received a message from him. As I sent too many messages like "Anna, pick up, pick up, come on line".*

"What happened Adheera?"

"Why didn't you come online?"

"I had a meeting dear"

"Ok, come to the church which is backside of the Park".

"Why?"

"Please, I have something for you".

"Ok, I'll come and meet before I leave this town".

*I could not sleep a whole night.*

*Once the Sun has arisen, I got up from the bed and was ready to go to Church with her.*

*"Happy Birthday Akka"*

*"Thank you sweet heart"*

*We went to church together. When she was in prayer I came out. He was standing under the tree and waiting for me.*

*"Anna, Can I see her photo?"*

*When he showed that photo, my hands started shivering and tears were running out of my eyes.*

*"She is", I hugged him and cried.*

*"What happened Adheera?"*

*"I told you that I would let your sadness away from your heart."*

*"Yes."*

*"I am going to do that".*

*When Janaki came out from the church, she sensed the smell of Vijay's soul. When she was distributing hand full of chocolates to the children, I held his hands and took him to her.*

*"Akka!"*

*When she turned back to Adheera, Vijay was shocked to see her with a stick in her hand and* glasses on her face. He was half dead to see her like that.

"Janaki!", he was numb.

"Vijay!", she slowly moved her hands towards his face.

"Hey, What happened to you Janaki?"

"Vijay, are you completely alright?".

"Janaki, answer me What happened to your eyes?"

She dropped the stick and sat.

"On that day fighting, you were hurt almost... Remember you got hurt on your eyes, I didn't want you to lose your vision, so..."

*"So", his words stammered.*

*"I gave mine", she said.*

*"Why did you leave me then?, I was searching for you as a child who lost his mother.", He hugged her tightly and cried like a child.*

*"I never wanted the pain of losing anyone again."*

*"I was scared and my heart was pierced into pieces, when I saw you in that state, I was dead actually.", her words and hands shivered.*

*"Why did you do that Janaki?" He cried.*

*"Vijay... that is what people do when they love someone deeply".*

*"Don't leave me again please, I can't live a second without you anymore Janaki".*

*"Vijay…"*

*Suddenly Vijay goes on his knees and asked, "Will you allow me to be your vision? Please don't say no, all I want to do is be by your side always"*

*Janaki took her hands near his cheeks.*

*"Vijay"*

*He held her closer to him and looked at her with his eyes full of love and kisses her on her forehead.*

*"Janaki, Happy Birthday!".*

*"How cute they are!" my eyes became wet with happiness to see them together.*

*"Soulful love always sparkles!"*